Brian Hales: The Complete Polygamy Interview

I0419395

Table of Contents

Introduction

Gospel Tangents needs your support. Please consider donating to our website, https://GospelTangents.com in any amount. We will use your donation, and the information from these podcasts to produce professional Mormon History Documentaries and other resources such as this.

Rick Bennett of Gospel Tangents sat down with Brian Hales to discuss Mormon polygamy during Joseph Smith's lifetime. Transcripts of the interviews were previous published as a series of interviews. This edition combines the entire 2 hour interviews into a single book.

(Note this conversation was recorded on April 26, 2017 in Layton, Utah. I will use GT for Gospel Tangents to indicate when I am talking to Brian. The interview has been lightly edited to remove verbal miscues.)

Canadian Polygamy – Should it be Legal?

The Interview

GT: Well I'd like to welcome everybody out here to *Gospel Tangents Podcast*. I'm really excited to talk to Dr. Brian Hales. He's *the* expert on polygamy, or one of the experts I guess. I'm grateful to have you here and thank you for letting me take some of your time today.

Brian: Rick it's really a privilege for me to be here.

GT: Well thanks. One of the things I'd like to do is to introduce you to my audience a little bit. Typically I try to talk to a lot of historians who are doctors but you are the first physician, although I have talked to a physician's assistant as well. Could you tell us a little bit about your background, even in medicine? I think you're a Utah man. Is that right?

Brian: I am actually. I went to Utah State, grew up in Logan and got a medical degree from University of Utah, so I have a little bit of the Ute blood in me as well.

GT: Aggie and Utah, ok.

Brian: Aggies primarily. Then I had a member of my family who was involved with Mormon fundamentalism and that kind of steered me over into thinking about polygamy. This is back in 1989 so it's been quite some time ago. At that point I was in a residency for anesthesia and I do tell people that my books are part of my full anesthesia services. You've probably heard me say that joke, but I got interested then in Mormon fundamentalism and published a book, co-authored a book in 1991 dealing with that topic but then later a couple of other books.

People were asking me about Joseph Smith's polygamy, and I didn't have answers and really I would argue none of the books did. Todd Compton's book has some things that were very helpful but he had written biographies and it wasn't focused specifically on Joseph, so there was still a lot of room for research and to also try to figure out some of the historical aspects that really were just big question marks I think in a lot of people's minds.

So in 2006-2007 I hired Don Bradley who is a dear friend but also a remarkable researcher and he went out and did a lot of research for me, gathered documents, and I told him to get everything: anti-Mormon or supportive, whatever he could find. We wanted to get every known document, and it was interesting because after we had been going about six months, it became obvious that if we kept going, eventually we would be able to put either a transcript or at least a reference to every known document on polygamy within the volumes that we were putting together. So we got kind of excited about that but that was mostly Don Bradley's work. But his help, I put together three volumes (vol 1[1], vol 2[2], vol 3[3]) on polygamy. There's been a few new things come out. This was in 2013 that they were published, but not a lot has come out but a few very important things that we can talk about.

GT: Yeah we'll definitely want to talk about that. Well great! I'm glad you talked about how you got interested in fundamentalist Mormonism, I guess. There are different branches. Could you just kind of briefly give a sketch of the main ones? I guess we've got the FLDS, AUB. Are there

---

[1] Can be purchased at http://amzn.to/2q7UfpF
[2] Can be purchased at http://amzn.to/2pOQDWg
[3] Can be purchased at http://amzn.to/2q7MU9v

any others? Could you kind of give a background on Mormon fundamentalism?

Brian: Well do you mind if I just talk about what's going on in Canada right now?

GT: Sure, that would be great.

Brian: I just got back last week, it was a week ago today from Cranbrook, [British Columbia,] Canada. That is where they are holding a trial right now for two leading polygamists: Winston Blackmore and James Oler. The Canadian government has kind of a different system than we have here in the United States in that they have a law against polygamy. It's been on the books since 1899 or before. They haven't prosecuted anybody in the last 100 plus years, but what they are able to do in Canada that we don't do in the U.S. is they can petition their Supreme Court to rule on the constitutionality of a particular law. In 2012 they did this to the state, well it would be the province, British Columbia did a provincial court saying, is this polygamy law constitutional? They ruled that it was.

They are now prosecuting the two leading polygamists because there's a group of hundreds, not thousands, but hundreds located about an hour, hour and a half away from Cranbrook where the court's being held. So the prosecution, the attorneys called me up and said, would you come up and be an expert? They said, we don't want you to testify for or against, and I told them that isn't what I'm interested in doing. They wanted somebody to give an accurate history which is something that I had studied.

I can even give you a copy of a chart that I've updated and you can put it the show notes or however you do online if people are interested. It's available at https://mormonfundamentalism.com, but they asked me to come up and start with Joseph Smith and go right through on authority to the 1890 and 1904 manifestos, the period between that and the fundamentalist groups coming together at the end of the 1920s, and then the branches and the breakoffs and I put together a nice little chart that talks about the different groups and of course the fundamentalists up there. The polygamists up there are, or were aligned with the FLDS, but in 2002 Winston Blackmore was excommunicated by Warren Jeffs over kind of an interesting situation where Warren, representing his father Rulon who had had strokes and was not necessarily communicating that much but Warren gave the word that Winston was supposed to actually take the life of a woman who had been involved with what he felt was a transgression within their religious beliefs and Winston refused to do it so he was excommunicated. This was before Warren had actually taken over.

James Oler is the other leader and when Winston was excommunicated as the bishop up there then James Oler took over. [It was] kind of a sad tale. My heart actually goes out to both of these guys. I don't agree with their polygamy but the sad thing is that James Oler helped with that 2012 case where they brought up the constitutionality of the anti-polygamy law, and James Oler was just a friend of the court, or gave an opinion on that, and then it came out against the polygamists and Warren was unhappy with that and sent him out to repent from afar which takes away his wives and everything. He seems like a really nice guy. I only chatted with him, exchanged very few words but he seemed like a very humble man and again I want it known that I am not up there to testify against the polygamists. There's been some people saying that. It isn't true. I was totally neutral on that.

Rick I don't know if you want to know this but personally I don't think that we should allow polygamy either in Canada or the United States, but my reason might be a little surprising to you, because in a country or government that allows same-sex marriage, and again I'm not speaking for or against that, but if we allow same-sex marriage and we allow polygamy, you could have networks of people, hundreds of people all married to each other in a variety of ways.

If the government privileged marriage, in other words if a married man and a married woman, whatever kind of marriage it is, if they have a privilege a single person doesn't have, then everybody's going to want to be married in some way. I think it would force the government to basically get out of the marrying business and leave it as a social construct or a religious agreement. But in doing that it would also take away any privilege for marriage which I think could harm the family. So that's my reasoning for saying I don't think we should have legal polygamy. I think a society can absorb polygamy on a small scale. It obviously can't be practiced widely because of the differences in people, male and female, the gendered differences of being born, but I don't think a society can absorb both of the expansions or marriage at the same time. I mean you can do same-sex marriage, or you can do polygamy. I don't think it's good for the family to do both.

Does D&C 132 Conflict with JST Genesis?

The Interview

GT: In your book, you've got a three volume set I guess I should say, and one of the other things I wanted to talk about was, I had an interview with Dr. Mark Staker. I don't know if you were able to watch those interviews? (video here[4])

Brian: Just a part of it.

GT: Ok, in one of those interviews with Dr. Mark Staker, he really surprised me when he said that he thought that Black Pete, who was the first black Mormon in the church, baptized just six months after [the church was organized], may have introduced polygamy to Kirtland, which kind of blew my mind. I'd never heard that before, and I wanted—you know you're kind of an expert on Kirtland era polygamy and that as well. I wanted to get your opinion on that point.

Brian: You know Mark, who is a remarkable scholar and you don't dismiss anything that someone who's done his level of research comes up with, you don't dismiss it just out of hand. You want to entertain it and see how it fits with the other building blocks, but Mark and I have actually exchanged emails and had conversations and we actually have some disagreements on a number of points.

I am aware of this from your podcast, and I think that Joseph Smith didn't need Black Pete to introduce him to polygamy, the idea. We see this all the time with say the Book of Mormon. Critics will say Joseph got this idea of Noah in Mosiah. Noah is actually this person in Joseph's life and they'll try to draw these parallels and things. It's interesting talk but I don't think it's all that necessary.

---

4 See https://www.youtube.com/watch?v=19lxpBdzWKs&t

Joseph knew the Old Testament, he knew Abraham had more than one wife and Jacob, so why would we need to think that it was Black Pete that was introducing this in a very real way, especially when Joseph wasn't supportive of so much that was going on when he first arrived down there, and the types of spiritual experiences that they were expressing in their church meetings and things like that. So I'm a little dubious on that, but I just applaud Mark. I say go forward and let us know.

The timeline lines up pretty well with Joseph having been translating the Old Testament, particularly the discussion about the patriarchs who were polygamists in 1831 when we also having them talking about marrying Lamanites if we believe W. W. Phelps [account of] revelation that he recounted decades later, so I think that the chronology of him bringing up the question as he's translating fits the evidence a little bit better, but with Mark Staker, he may have other evidence I haven't seen. We'll just have to wait for it.

GT: Yeah, well Mark did admit that it was more of a circumstantial case, so not strong evidence, but he said Black Pete was seen as an Indian which he was black, but whatever. He said early in the Mormon Church they said, well you're black. You must know what Indians are all about so that was kind of how it started and Indians are polygynous and he thought maybe that might have been something, so anyway, interesting thought I had never heard before.

Let's go back to that timeline because Black Pete, the record only shows him from about 1830-1831 which is the time period if you read section 132 in the Doctrine and Covenants[5] it says that portions of the revelation may have been received as early as then. Mark said well it could have been Black Pete that maybe tried to influence polygamy

---

[5] See https://www.lds.org/scriptures/dc-testament/dc/132

among the Kirtland saints, and that may have been why Joseph turned to the Bible and looked at polygamy and Abraham as you mentioned. So my question is, well there's a few questions.

One of the interesting things, and I'm just going to reveal my opinion. Polygamy is one of the most difficult topics for me to wrestle with theologically. As we look at, let's talk about *Doctrine and Covenants 132*. It says in there that God gave Abraham the wives. It seems to me if Joseph Smith is translating the Book of Genesis, or retranslating it, and he made some changes in the Book of Genesis, if you read that story in Genesis, it seems pretty clear that it wasn't God, it was Sarah that said, Abraham, why don't you take Hagar? {Brian nods}. It seems to me if Joseph Smith is translating that, wouldn't there have been a revelation there or a Joseph Smith Translation? He leaves that story basically unchanged. Do you have any comments on that?

Brian: There's at least a couple of ways that could be interpreted at least in my view. There are people who say Joseph knew all of section 132 in 1831. I'm not one who believes that at all.

I believe that he may have learned in 1831 that plural marriage was a correct principle, and that's kind of the language some of the brethren used. He learned it was a correct principle. In other words Abraham wasn't sinning or transgressing by practicing polygamy. The Bible does not teach anything about whether polygamy is good or bad. All we know is that Abraham practiced it and Abraham was a friend of God. We can get that from scriptures, so Joseph may have just gone with his question about is this a valid practice? What was the second question?

GT: Joseph Smith Translation leaves that biblical story unchanged...

Brian: Right.

GT: ..but in D&C 132 it says God gave the wives.

Brian: The other thing is that in the Bible there's nobody commanded to practice polygamy ever, but we have in section 132 that Abraham was commanded by God to marry Hagar. So I don't think Joseph knew any of this in 1831. If we follow Joseph's teachings even on something like eternal marriage, we find a hint of it in 1835 but still there's nothing there, and I'm not sure, and I think Mark would disagree with me on this, Mark Staker, but I don't think Joseph was fully apprised of the authority and what it could do that he received in the temple on April 3, 1836 from Elijah, Moses, and Elias. I honestly am not sure that he understood that authority until maybe some years later, but that's speculation on my part. We certainly don't have him teaching anything about plural marriage or eternal marriage until we get into Nauvoo in late 1840, early 1841. Did I cover that?

GT: Well so I guess my question is as far as 132 and Genesis, does it seem to you that there's a difference among those two scriptures as far as whether God commanded Hagar to be a plural wife or whether Sarah was totally responsible?

Brian: And because Genesis, even the Joseph Smith Translation states that...

GT interrupts: Yeah it leaves that story unchanged.

Brian: ...Sarah was the driver and not God through Abraham.

GT agrees: Uh huh.

Brian: I believe all of these principles came to Joseph line upon line, precept upon precept. Some of the exciting things that are happening down at BYU, Tom Wayment and others are looking at the Joseph Smith Translation very carefully and discovering that it really shouldn't be thought of as actual scripture in and of itself, that it was a chance for Joseph to expand upon the text to make the Bible text correspond with the theology that he was receiving through revelation, or through communications that he portrayed to be from God. So for me to see the JST Genesis and that it doesn't necessarily say what comes in 1843 doesn't surprise me because of the line upon line, precept upon precept process.

GT: Ok.

Polygamy Rumors – Declaration on Marriage

The Interview

GT: Clair Barrus gave a presentation at a Mormon history conference in which he said that there was no documentation of any polygamy revelations prior to, I wish I remembered this exactly, but I believe 1838. There's no documentation of that until about 1838 and that's when you get the first points of documentation. In talking with Dr. Staker, one of the things he mentioned was, I believe it was 1835, you have the *Declaration on Marriage* which was originally a section in the *Book of Commandments*, but then it was later taken out and replaced with section 132. Could you talk about some of those polygamy rumors?

I know in your book you said there was nothing in the news[papers] about them. In 1835, Dr. Staker makes the case, well why would they talk about polygamy if polygamy wasn't a problem? There must have been something going on in Kirtland in the early, at least 1830s.

Brian: The first accusation against the Latter-day Saints, they weren't called that then, against the Mormons, the Mormonites, that they had embraced some alternate form of marriage, came in 1831. It was in conjunction with the Law of Consecration and it was basically not only do they share everything, they share wives. That was the accusation that came up.

Of course it's easily refuted. There's nothing to support that it was even thought of or discussed. So when people say they were talking about polygamy in Kirtland, I would really like to see the data on that, that this was really a response to polygamy because my research shows that there was, with respect to Joseph and Fanny Alger, discussion of adultery and that was the claim that everybody was worried about. I don't find anybody discussing polygamy during that period.

If we read the section 101, which is "On Marriage" it was entitled, it talks about polygamy but it talks about fornication and adultery, and so to say that this is reacting to polygamy rumors, it could be true but there is no evidence for that, and so I argue that this is really just a blanket statement that's covering the comments made about this idea of Law of Consecration of sharing wives, as well as any other accusations and Oliver Cowdery wrote a very nice declaration. He said we haven't got anywhere near enough time to respond to all of the accusations that are being made against us, so I don't think that's a real strong argument, that the article because it mentions a man having one wife, and technically the language, if you look at it closely does not prevent polygamy. We can talk about that if you want. This is not my observation, this is an observation from the RLDS Church writer, as well as President Joseph F. Smith, that the language does not actually prevent polygamy. It's a little ambiguous when it comes to that.

GT: Actually go ahead. I was just reading that just yesterday, but go ahead and finish that point.

Brian: Ok, what it says is that a man should have but one—a woman should have but one husband, and a man....

GT interrupts: A man one wife.

Brian: ...One wife. {Brian looks for a book} The language doesn't say should be *only* one wife or at least one wife. I could pull up the exact...

GT interrupts: Yeah go ahead and grab it.

{break}

Brian: Ok what I have now is the 1835 *Doctrine & Covenants* and what it says here, it says

> "The Church of Christ has been reproached with the crime of fornication and polygamy. We declare that we believe that one man should have one wife, and one woman but one husband."

What has been pointed out is that it doesn't say that a man should have *only* one wife. It doesn't say that a man should have *at least* one wife, and so the accusation has been made by critics and even by a church president that this was intentional language allowing for polygamy to be practiced in the future.

Now the irony of that is this was printed twice in Nauvoo as evidence that the church was not practicing polygamy. So despite this loophole, potential loophole, do I think that Joseph put that in intentionally? I have no idea. It wouldn't surprise me if he did, to be honest with you. He had a long view things and he would have known, he may have known again that at least it was a correct principle from 1831, so whether it was carefully crafted, or just a coincidence. If you want to disagree, and that goes for anyone listening, that's fine, because we'll never resolve this.

GT: Well one other point I want to talk about, Dr. Staker mentioned, and I believe Dr. Richard Bennett mentioned as well some people believe that that section was not authored by Joseph Smith but was authored by Oliver Cowdery. What's your opinion on that?

Brian: You know in my volume one, I go into this in some detail, and what we find is yes Joseph was gone, and yes they were quick to get this passed. In fact they called for this conference on Sunday to be done on Monday and there were almost no leaders there. The Quorum of the Twelve there were almost no one present, the High Council really weren't represented. The theory is that they were trying to get it pushed through before Joseph got back because Oliver had these reasons and stuff.

I don't think so and I'm grateful for Michael Marquardt for helping me. We sat one afternoon down in his basement and we went through all the documents, and what we find is at that at point in time they needed to go forward with printing the *Doctrine & Covenants*. They had published we think most of the book up to section 101, which is the *Article on Marriage* and that they're having piles of all these papers around the printing office. So we think, or at least I think and I think Michael agrees that the driver at that point was really that they just wanted to get official approval so that they could finish publishing the *Doctrine & Covenants* and so I don't think that they were trying to do something backhanded with Joseph.

When Joseph came back there's no evidence that he really disapproved of what had happened. In fact he quotes or refers to the *Article on Marriage* two or three times later when he is performing marriages. He said this declares our church's belief which they had to have in writing in order for the elders of the church to be authorized by the state to perform state recognized marriages, so there were a number of things.

The other evidence that I found is that if you go back and look at the index of the 1835 Doctrine & Covenants which was written weeks before Joseph had left Kirtland, you find that section 101 is referenced in this index, so the index was written before and Joseph even quotes from the index, but the index didn't have page numbers. So I think that information tells me that yes they were planning to include it. Joseph was planning to include it and it was just a matter of getting the printing done so they'd have a page number to put in there. But people can try this out themselves. Just get an 1835 copy of the *Doctrine and Covenants* and look at it. We know it was published earlier because of the timeline of some of the things that were quoted from it.

I don't ascribe to—it's actually I think Richard Van Wagoner's book, Mormon Polygamy[6] that first introduced this theory. Todd Compton reiterated the possibility. He didn't jump totally on board, but I really think that it's a...

GT interrupts: So whether Oliver may have authored it or not, it didn't seem like it bothered Joseph at all and he was fine with it. Is that safe to say?

Brian: I believe so. I'd have to refresh my memory, but what we do know is he could have had it rescinded but he also quoted it as authoritative and Michael Marquardt pointed this out to me I think he's even published that somewhere that Joseph did consider it after the fact to be the official declaration of the church at that time.

GT: Ok.

---

[6] Can be purchased at http://amzn.to/2pbiKCe

1st Plural Wife Fanny Alger: Time or Eternity Polygamy?

The Interview

GT: Alright, well let's move on to his first polygamist wife. Now you said Fanny Al-gurr. I've heard lots of people say Fanny Al-jerr. Is there a correct way to say that?

Brian: A family member said it was All-gurr.

GT: All-gurr.

Brian: And I never know how it's going to come out of my mouth. I mean just because they said it All-gurr now doesn't mean they said it All-gurr back then. It's spelled so it could be pronounced in any number of ways and I try to remember to say All-gurr but who knows how they said it?

GT: Alright. Well why don't you kind of give us a brief overview for those of us people who may not be familiar with the story of Fanny. How did she know Joseph and how did they get acquainted and that sort of thing?

Brian: You've already talked to Mark Staker and he's the one I'm dependent upon to try to identify when Fanny actually arrived in Kirtland, because some people want to pair Joseph and Fanny as early as 1831 and all. Mark told me that he thinks it couldn't have been any, that Fanny did not joined the Smith family as a domestic in their household until at the earliest late 1833 and probably it was 1834.

We have one witness, one testimonial, only one so do with it as you please that remembers Joseph saying the angel came in July of 1834, Mary Elizabeth Rollins years later, many years later remembering this, but for me I believe Joseph would not have entered into plural marriage prior to that time, so I place the Fanny Alger-Joseph Smith union, and I believe it was a plural marriage for a couple of reasons like I'll explain in 1835, probably late 1835, maybe early 1836. I don't think they would have been able to keep it secret from Emma for very long. To me it's implausible that they could have been married and actually having relations which may have occurred. There's some evidence supporting that. We just don't know, but they couldn't have done this for very long without Emma figuring it out. She's a smart lady.

I put the marriage late 1835, early 1836 discovered a few weeks or months later, but that timeline is completely controversial. People are willing to pick dates earlier, weeks/months earlier than that timeline but I don't think that it actually would have been much earlier than that.

GT: Ok, so then what brought the relationship to light?

Brian: Well I meant to say there's a couple reasons I think it was a marriage rather than just an adulterous relationship. We have one account, a single attestation again from a rather dubious source, Mosiah Hancock added a description on the end of his father's autobiography where he describes how Levi Hancock was approached by Joseph and Joseph said "Levi, I want to marry Fanny so can you be an intermediary in this?"

This was a pattern that was repeated in Nauvoo, not always but it happened. Levi approached Fanny. Fanny said yes, so Levi performed the marriage. It wouldn't have been a sealing, it wouldn't have been an eternal marriage, but the authority that was used by Joseph to marry people for the church but just for time in Kirtland, that authority certainly could have been used here, and that's my theory. Again these are unanswerable questions and critics are quick to rush in with other alternative interpretations.. It's just insoluble.

GT: So let me make sure I understand that. So the marriage seems to have occurred before the vision in 1836 of Elias, Elijah, and the third person.

Brian: Moses.

GT: Moses.

Brian: Yeah.

GT: So you're telling me that the marriage to Fanny was probably performed for time only?

Brian: There are some who believe it was after April 3rd.

GT: That the marriage occurred after the vision.

Brian: Yeah. You actually can plug that in. It's plausible. Don Bradley's done some really good research and he dates the discovery to I think it's June, May-June of 1836, so if the marriage occurred in say late April, May-June and lasted just a few months before Emma found out, which is entirely plausible, I don't know that I embrace that, but Don at least we know when it broke up. We can date that pretty well, then it could have been a sealing. The authority could have been sealing authority that Joseph would have given to Levi.

An alternate interpretation, and this is a question that comes up a lot Rick, it's a good question. If it wasn't a sealing, then what authority was used? The state wasn't going to allow Joseph to marry a second wife, so the only

21

authority that it could have been would be priesthood authority and Joseph was already using that authority to marry people just for time there in Kirtland. So one interpretation is Joseph gave that authority to Levi and this would have been strictly a priesthood marriage that Joseph would have argued God recognized and so if he recognized it and Fanny and her family apparently recognized it as did others who were involved, but not Oliver [Cowdery] and not Emma.

But the other reason that I think this was an actual marriage and ceremony was performed was that Eliza Snow moved in in early 1836 to live with the Smiths and teach their children. In 1887, he was an independent historian, Andrew Jensen showed up at Eliza's door and said I'm trying to make a list of all of the wives of Joseph Smith. He had been down to see Melissa Lott and Melissa Lot had given him thirteen names that he'd written down on this piece of paper and at some point instead of him writing down what Eliza was saying, he turned the paper over to her and gave her the pencil, and she wrote an additional thirteen names, and among those names were Fanny Alger.

So my theory is that if this had been an adulterous relationship, and he also wrote a paper on Fanny where he quotes Eliza as saying she was well-acquainted with Fanny, and that Fanny was the one that Emma made such a fuss about, so Eliza was there and I think Eliza would have known the details of what was going on. She considered Fanny a wife and so these two bits of evidence to me I think are convincing for me that this was in fact a marriage, probably not a sealing, and again I place it to late '35, early '36 but there's really no way to date it.

GT: Yeah that's interesting. I'm going to reference Dr. Staker again, one more time. One of the things Dr. Staker said which was surprising to me and I wanted to get your opinion on was he said that he thought that when Peter, James, and John came in 1829 or 1830, and restored the Melchizedek Priesthood to Joseph and Oliver, that they gave the sealing power to Joseph then. If you read the book of Matthew [16:18-19] it says basically Upon Peter—I'm not quoting it right but he gave the sealing power to Peter. Upon this rock I build my church and whatever you seal on earth shall be sealed in heaven.

So I guess there's a case that could be made when Joseph received the Melchizedek Priesthood from Peter, James, and John, do you think that sealing power might have come as early as 1830, or was it really 1836 with Elias, Elijah, and Moses?

Brian: You know it's a super question because Brigham Young later said that if you have the apostleship, you have all the authority, and the senior apostle of course holds the keys to exercising all of the authority, but every apostle has all the authority. There's no other authority that could be granted except that given to an apostle, and we're told that Peter, James, and John ordained them as apostles with the same calling that Paul had received, and Paul was an apostle. So that's another supportive argument for this.

But there seems to be in the economy of heaven and authority, a need for certain keys to be restored to unlock certain authority, and you could theorize that they had the authority but they didn't have the keys. Now it gets really messy really quick and I don't know of anybody who's really tried to sort through all of this in a way that we could consider it an orthodox teaching.

GT: That's actually what Mark said. He had the authority, he didn't have the keys until 1836.

Brian: Oh, well it that's what Mark said that's a really good thing then. I'm feeling really good because Mark's looked into this a lot more than I have.

GT: Ok, very interesting.

Fanny Alger Part 2: Plural Marriage or Adultery?

The Interview

GT: Alright, let's go on. Somehow this relationship was discovered. You alluded to Emma wasn't very pleased with it and neither was Oliver Cowdery. Can you talk about their reactions and how they discovered it?

Brian: Yes. {reaching for book} In an appendix here in my volume two, and I'm not trying to plug my books. They're out in paperback now.

GT: You can plug away.

Brian: Can I plug?

GT: I'm perfectly fine with that. They're great books.

Brian: I'll just hold this up to the camera. I think I have actually posted this appendix on https://MormonPolygamyDocuments.org. If you go there, I think I actually have put this up there. The point is there's only 19 accounts that we have that talk about Fanny. They contradict each other. They come from good sources and dubious sources. If somebody wants to figure out what they want to believe about Fanny, just get that appendix, read the 19 accounts and form your own opinion. There are actually a few others that have important things, but those are the primary accounts that people need to know.

What we understand is that more or less, the people that Joseph Smith told about Fanny Alger as a plural wife, they didn't believe him. But most of the people that learned it from Fanny did believe which is interesting. Fanny's family believed. The family that Fanny went to live with was Chauncey Webb and Eliza Jane Webb, they believed that this was an actual marriage, but Joseph is caught with Fanny and they're in a haymow, they're in a barn, and we were out there in Kirtland with the John Whitmer Historical Association meeting this last September, and I asked Mark, 'where is the barn?' He had no idea. It's long since been destroyed.

They were discovered by Emma "in the act." We could assume that was something sexual. Some people want to say it was in the act of getting married by Levi, the ceremony. It's a bit of a stretch. Maybe he was in the act of something affectionate. Virtually anything affectionate would have been over the line in Emma's eyes understandably. She caught them, and she's not accepting Joseph's explanation at all.

'This is a plural marriage. God authorized it.'

'Yeah right. She's pretty and this isn't working for me.'

Joseph, according to one of the accounts gets Oliver and says in the middle of the night. 'Oliver, come help me with this.' Oliver hears the story and sides with Emma and thinks Joseph is having an adulterous affair. That was his opinion, probably right up until his death, that Joseph was not authorized to marry her. It wasn't a marriage. He made hints to members of the high council that Joseph had been guilty of adultery. He did not accept any story of a marriage ceremony as being valid, and neither did Emma.

Years later in 1847, William McLellin had an interview with Emma, and Emma didn't want to talk about polygamy but she did say look. If you tell me things you heard, I'll tell you whether they're true or false, and in that conversation she said Joseph was both an adulterer and a polygamist. We don't know what she meant by that. My theory is that she never did accept Fanny as a true plural marriage. She thought it was adultery. Joseph had to seek repentance and all that. In my mind, that's the dichotomy. She accepted Nauvoo polygamy but never accepted Kirtland polygamy.

GT: So going back to that other point that I just made. I didn't realize that Oliver sided with Emma. That's kind of interesting. Oliver's opinion, would that argue against the 1830 sealing power restoration and more towards an 1836, or do you think that has any impact on that at all?

Brian: Do you know, I do personally believe even though Oliver was there receiving this authority from Elijah, Moses, and Elias, I really am not convinced that they knew what this authority was all about. Of course there was a rift right after that. The blowup came in, according to Don [Bradley], it was just weeks later. From that point forward, there's a rift between Joseph and Oliver. If Joseph was receiving additional understanding about the authority, Oliver would not have been privy to any of that. So the only knowledge Oliver had of those ordinations was what they had before that point and whatever was given in that vision, which apparently wasn't much, or if it was, it wasn't written down. So again, I can see Oliver receiving authority he doesn't understand and then there's a rift and he never does gain any understanding. Joseph in fact receives additional revelation during the next four or five years that helped him understand it.

GT: Well that revelation in 1836 wasn't written down for 40 years, so it definitely took a while.

Brian: Well they did have it in third person written down.

GT: Oh, they did?

Brian: Yeah they do. People, the critics of the church don't attack the timeline associated with the April 3, 1836 revelation. It was recorded. That is lost. It was turned into third person for the history just within days by I think Warren Parrish. That account we do have. In fact it was published in the *Ensign* by Elder Marlin K. Jensen, when he was there, so you can see it there. It's in third person, and that was changed.

GT: Ok, so it wasn't canonized for 40 years but it was written down right away.

Brian: Right.

GT: Ok, Great. So what happened to Fanny? Do you know when it was discovered and what happened to Fanny after?

Brian: It's an interesting story and I'm not that expert on it, but Don has them being discovered, I think it's June of 1836, and Emma throws her out of the house, understandably. She goes to live with Chauncey Webb for a matter of weeks or maybe months until her family who lived in the northern part of the state are able to come down and pick her up. And they, by September, they're on their way out.

Then there's this funny story, and I think it's from Mosiah Hancock where Fanny was being held captive in the Kirtland Temple. Joseph sent Levi to free her out of the Kirtland Temple. He backs his wagon up to the temple and she jumps from the window. If you look at the heights involved, it just doesn't work. Mosiah Hancock is not that reliable. He's got some really weird stories.

28

There's the story of there being a big to-do about it and they leave in September.

They go to Missouri as their destination but they stop in Indiana. There Fanny marries a guy named Solomon Custer. Don theorizes that Fanny is pregnant, and that's why she jumps into this marriage so quickly. I'm not sure I believe that to be so, but we can understand why she would, having been broken up with Joseph—Joseph could grant a priesthood divorce as easily as he could allow for the priesthood marriage. Some people say she couldn't have been married to Joseph because she got remarried so quickly. I don't know that I buy that. I think when they left Joseph could have said goodbye and that would have been the end of the relationship.

Her marrying this Solomon Custer who was apparently a really good guy, not very religious, and they settled there in Indiana where she lived out the rest of her life. She joined the Universalist Church, had I think eight children and died a member of Universalist Church. We have some interesting stories. There's one story that after Joseph was killed, he had told Brigham, 'I want you to marry all of my plural wives to make sure that they are taken care of.' There is one rumor, and I don't know what to think of it that says Brigham actually went up and told Fanny that he would marry her, even though she was already married, just to fulfill the letter of this law that Joseph allegedly told the Twelve.

But the story doesn't say that Fanny was offended and threw him out of the house, but has her just responding that 'I want to be the wife of one husband,' and sent Brigham on his way. I don't know if that's true. We have a little more reliable story from Benjamin Johnson who said that Fanny's brother had approached her and asked

29

her about her relationship with Joseph Smith, in the marriage. Her response was simply, 'that's all my own affair,' and didn't say anything elaborate on it.

Her family, Fanny's family went to Nauvoo. The Webbs with whom she lived went to Nauvoo. They followed the church west. Whatever actually happened between Joseph and Fanny did not bother their faith of these people who knew the details, same with Eliza Snow.

GT: Was it true that her parents came all the way to Utah?

Brian: Her brother did and I don't know if they died or all, but they didn't leave the church. It's interesting that John Alger in 1891, this is right after the 1890 Manifesto, he left the church over the Manifesto. He had a polygamist wife and he could not accept that. So again some irony.

GT: Fanny's brother was a polygamist?

Brian: Uh huh, and he left the church over the Manifesto of 1890.

GT: Wow I did not know that. That's interesting.

Brian: Yeah. I don't know how you want to read that, comparing it to 1835.

GT: That is very interesting.

What are the Theological Justifications for Polygamy?

The Interview

GT: Ok, so let's leave Fanny alone for a while. There was a big break in polygamist marriages. How long was that break, and who was the next wife?

Brian: Do you know there is some evidence for Joseph marrying plural wives between 1836 and 1841. I think it's dubious, but Fawn Brodie in her book No Man Knows My History[7] has several names there, but the evidence isn't totally clear that it didn't happen.

I don't believe it happened because in order for it to happen I think Joseph had to build up a little of the theology of sealing, so there just was no real timeline for this to happen. I mean Fawn Brodie's version is just full of problems. It's bad scholarship, her timeline and she's interpreting things wrong. But there's at least one quote saying that one of Joseph's wives was married, I think it was Lucinda Pendleton, I could be wrong, but was married before they got to Nauvoo. Again, no evidence to support that but one late recollection from somebody who wasn't even a member of the church at the time. For the most part, my interpretation is that there was no one. He was not involved with anyone in a plural marriage between 1836 and 1841.

GT: It would make sense he would take a break with Emma's reaction.

---

[7] Can be purchased at http://amzn.to/2teGu67

Brian chuckles: Well that was just what I was going to say. I mean Joseph probably got an ultimatum from Emma. If you ever do this again, we're done, or something because Emma was a strong personality. If she didn't accept this came from God, despite the revelations, despite the Book of Mormon, you can certainly understand why Joseph would have been reticent to jump back in. There's multiple accounts of him not wanting to do it. The critics ignore them as prevarications, but I think that he really didn't want to do it because he knew what Emma was going to say when she found out. Eventually she would.

We fast forward to 1840s, late 1840s and we find several people remembering. We're dealing with very late accounts at this point. There's been an article by Gary Bergera talking about how the marriages were actually in 1840. I think his reasoning is problematic and I've responded to that. I think we're very solidly in 1841. On April 5th, Joseph was sealed this time by Joseph B. Noble to his sister-in-law, and that was Louisa Beamon.

I will add that Don Bradley is doing some research now and he is actually pushing that marriage to April of '42. If you look at the chronology, it fits a lot better in April of '42 than 1841 because what we find is, except for Louisa, Joseph is marrying Zina Huntington and Prescinda Huntington and four or five women who all have legal husbands. Now we're getting into this polyandry question and my theory is that Joseph was just being sealed for eternity to these women, in the hopes that the angel who came a second time sometime prior to that—we don't have a date for the second visit of the angel commanding polygamy, but I theorize that he came and said "Do this." So Joseph was just doing these eternity only, non-sexual marriages because he was hoping to please the angel and also not offend Emma, who wouldn't have had to worry too much about them because there was no sexuality involved. The evidence is not absolutely conclusive, but I think there is a lot of reasons to believe that this is actually happening.

GT: So I'm glad you went there, because I wanted to talk about polyandry. I know that Dr. Lawrence Foster said that we shouldn't use that term. We should use a "proxy husband" which would make sense if there were no sexual relations. It does make you wonder why are they doing these in the first place? Why would an angel command you to marry somebody, and not have sexual relations because it does in D&C 132, it does say that one of the purposes is to raise up seed. So if you're not having sexual relations, why would an angel command such a thing?

Brian: It's a good question. Sometimes the critics will say, "that's the only reason" is to multiply and replenish. It's verse 63, but actually section 132 gives four reasons for plural marriage, and that's one of them. But I think there's another one that's much more important. Let me talk about the other two before we get to the most important one. It's a part of the restoration of all things, and I'm blocking on the third one.

The fourth one, the one that is the most important is that, and it takes a little bit of history, but Joseph asks God about polygamy in verse one. Then we find polygamy isn't mentioned until verse 32, 34. But what we find is the answer to the question about polygamy is that God is talking about eternal marriage. Verse seven talks about one man who has the keys. Verses eight through eighteen gives us three examples about what happens to associations or marriages that are not sealed by the authority of that one man. There's three examples there.

When does God give us examples? He's trying to teach a principle here.

Even in verse eighteen he's telling us if a man and a woman are married for time and all eternity, but if that marriage is not through the one man that holds the keys, it's not valid neither in force when they are out of the world. The Lord is putting three exclamation points behind verse seven that says there's one man on earth at a time that has this authority. Then in verses 19-20 it tells us of a monogamous couple who live worthily and are sealed by this authority, then they are exalted. They become gods. Their marriage continues after death. But it's talking just about a monogamous marriage through all of this, but in verses 16-17 it tells us that if a person dies, and they are not sealed by this authority, then they remain singly and separately, without exaltation in their saved condition to all eternity, telling us that every person will need to be sealed into eternal marriage. So plural marriage could ostensibly allow every worthy person, assuming there are more worthy women than men, and I've heard that that's a problem for some people, but go into any Christian congregation, or Mormon congregation and just look at the genders. There's always more women than men. Always.

This is a principle that reaches beyond death. It's far more important in my mind than multiply and replenish the earth. I was just going to look up the third reason here {looking in a book}.

[Break]

GT: Tell us about the four reasons in the Doctrine & Covenants for polygamy.

Brian: Just to reiterate, the easiest one is part of the restitution of all things, and if somebody asks you, "Why did Joseph do it?" The easy answer is, he was a prophet-restorer, and the old prophets did it, and he restored it. That's not entirely nuanced, and some would say it's even correct. I think it is generally.

The second one is it was a trial. This is the one I couldn't remember. It presented a special trial. The Lord does do that. It gives different people at different times different kinds of trials.

A third one was to—it was the one I had talked a great deal about. It allowed all men and women to enter into a marriage, even if this is a plural wife, and then the [fourth] one is the one we started with, multiply and replenish the earth.

Can I just add here Rick? There's been a book written lately that assumes that eternal polygamy is a bad thing. Of course on earth, polygamy is not fair. It's unequal. You could say it's sexist if you want, on earth. But I don't think that we know anything about eternal marriage, and we certainly don't know anything about eternal plural marriage. So to assume that that's a bad thing, that it victimizes women, and to assume that women should fear that is to fear unknown things.

God has promised us everlasting joy, a fullness of joy. His plan is a plan of happiness. I understand why even my own daughter is worried about this eternal polygamy idea. She's told her husband, "You're going to die before me because I'm not going to die before you and have you remarry so I'm a polygamist in heaven." She's told him that. I get that.

But at the same time, God has told us. This is not speculation. It's a fullness of joy. It's eternal happiness. It's exaltation for those who attain it. I think we just have to take faith in these things that are promises, and try not to fear the unknown. It may still be hard, and it is additional faith. I understand that, but I believe that whatever it is, and I have no desire to be a polygamist here or there. But I do believe that a woman is not going to feel victimized in eternity if she obtains exaltation. I think we just have to hold onto that faith, that that is true and then trust God. I don't agree with this idea that we know what eternal polygamy is and that we know that it is bad and that we should fear it here today.

Mormon Polyandry: More than One Husband

Introduction

When we talk about Mormon polygamy, we usually mean polygyny—the idea of a man has more than one wife. The opposite of that is polyandry, where a woman can have more than 1 husband. Did you know that Joseph Smith was sealed to women who were already legally married to other men? We're going to talk about one specific case in detail where Dr. Brian Hales believed that Joseph and Sylvia Session Lyon were parents of one of the offspring of Joseph Smith. He did a DNA test to find out if Joseph was the father of Josephine Lyon or if Windsor Lyon was the father. It's a pretty interesting story. I hope you'll check it out.

The Interview

GT: Alright, let's jump back. As we started this we started talking about Polyandry or proxy husbands. I know recently, I believe it was last year at Mormon History Association, you had said that you thought Joseph had sexual relations with Sylvia Sessions Lyon, if I remember the name right. DNA tests came back and that wasn't true. What are your opinions specifically on that marriage now as far as, were there sexual relations there, or not?

Brian: Do you know the evidence I will say is ambiguous. But for years, if you read my three volumes, I theorized that the marriage between Joseph Smith and Sylvia Sessions Lyon did include sexual relations in that plural marriage, and I had some theories as how that might have unfolded. When the DNA evidence came back—and part of the theory was that Joseph was the father of Josephine [daughter of Sylvia Sessions Lyon.] That's an important point. But when the DNA evidence came back that Windsor Lyon was the father, it required me to re-write things. I'll be honest with you. It wasn't what I expected, but it was what I had hoped.

It's a lot easier to understand Joseph Smith's plural marrying, particularly these sealings to already married women, it's a lot easier to understand them if he is not the father of Josephine. I argue that the evidence is ambiguous and that the facet if Joseph had actually practiced polyandry, he would have been so contrary to the Bible, there's really only one direct message. Paul mentions it once, and he condemns it as adultery. It's in Romans.

So the Bible condemns it, but it's also in frontier America, if a man is sexually involved with your wife, you can kill that man and the law's not going to go after you most of the time. We've got examples of that, clear up to...

GT: It happened with Parley P. Pratt [who was killed by a woman's husband.]

Brian: Exactly, Parley P. Pratt and others, where the law was just looking the other way. It was almost expected that either the husband, or if she wasn't married, a brother or father, but some other male relative would exact corporal punishment or capital punishment on the individual who committed this. So Joseph, if he had actually been involved with these men, he would have had to been 100% secret, worrying about his life if it was discovered, or have 100% complicity with the husband, which is not recorded in any case. Plus it would have been beyond novel. It would have been very controversial.

So I'm saying the little bit of ambiguous evidence that the critics have accumulated to say Joseph practiced it, and it is ambiguous. There's no unambiguous evidence saying that a woman ever believed she had two husbands in Nauvoo. We're not looking for a woman to say, "yeah I had sex with him and I had sex with him." That's not going to be found, but a woman, her family, a letter, or some other communication saying that a woman actually had two husbands or defending that idea, none of that is available. I'm arguing that if it were an actual teaching, it would have been defended and it would have been highly criticized by those who would have found it so repulsive they would have left the church or the critics would have picked up on it. We don't have anything.

So I'm arguing that ambiguous evidence on something that would have been explosive is not enough for me to say Joseph practiced sexual polyandry, and that's a term that I've used a lot in the past, but just a woman having more than one husband.

GT: So let's talk a little bit about that timeline with Sylvia Sessions Lyon. As I recall she married Windsor Lyon. They were married for a time. I believe Windsor got excommunicated or something {Brian nods.} So it was in this period where he was excommunicated that Joseph supposedly was sealed to Sylvia.

Brian: Right.

GT: Then perhaps they had sexual relations. I think you're telling me that's ambiguous. Is that what you're saying?

Brian: Right.

GT: Ok so then, well the question is was Josephine conceived while Joseph and Sylvia were married? That would therefore prove that he had sexual relations with her. It sounds like evidence says that no, it was with Windsor. So the conception must have happened after—well I'm a little confused on the timeline. Supposedly she got back together with Windsor so I believe, and please correct me if I'm wrong, I believe you said these were serial marriages, not polyandrous marriages in that she had two husbands. You're saying that she was married to Windsor, she was essentially religiously divorced, maybe not legally divorced, then she got back together with Windsor. Is that correct?

Brian: That's what I have written in my books, and what I've had to re-write.

GT: Oh, ok.

Brian: I don't believe that.

GT: You don't believe that anymore.

Brian: No I don't, but if somebody is interested, if you go on Youtube, before I gave my MHA presentation—what the MHA presentation does, it gives four interpretations of the new DNA evidence. One of them is polyandry, that's one of the four, and a second one was that there was no marriage at all, that they had no sealing or anything. Then I go through two others, I'd have to go back and look, but all of the possibilities I talk about, and the evidences supporting them. The one I came down against in that presentation, and before I gave it, I actually recorded it as a video, it's a 20 minute video. [See this video: https://www.youtube.com/watch?v=c9ceJMnXNxU]

GT: I do remember watching it but it's been a while.

Brian: Yeah. All the evidence, everything is there. It's still valid today. There's been nothing really new, though Don Bradley has been out doing more research and he hasn't found anything super helpful except that we do know that Josephine lived close, and there's a family tradition that says that her step-sister also lived close and she said she was present at the same time that Josephine was when Sylvia said that they are daughters of Joseph. The question is, are they daughters physically or are they daughters spiritually?

I had thought physically for Josephine but the argument is that they were both there, so it had to be spiritually. That may be a little confusing so I'll just lead you to refer people to that video and maybe they can hear all about it but the family tradition has been reinforced by some other things that Don Bradley has found out about their situations.

Family traditions are notorious for being false. Again, even though they've believed it for years doesn't mean that it's true, it just supports that interpretation which is that this was nothing more than a sealing. The language is that Sylvia was sealed to Joseph when Windsor was out of the church. Now if this were a polyandrous marriage, whether Windsor was out of the church or not would be unimportant. Who cares? Because if it's a polyandrous marriage, she's still having relations with him and then they get married and it would have no meaning.

But if Windsor is excommunicated, and it's in November 23rd, I think of 1842, then Sylvia can't be sealed to Windsor. So that would make perfect sense for her to seek out Joseph to be sealed to him just for the next life [in] an eternity only sealing. Right now Laura [Brian's wife] and I have gone through the evidence on these eleven polyandrous marriages. We think all of them were just for the next life.

Why the women chose Joseph over their legal husbands, sometimes these men were active Latter-day Saints, we don't know. It seems odd. But it's not as odd as them practicing actual sexual polyandry without anybody ever talking about it or finding that to be controversial.

GT: Ok, so your opinion is of all the eleven polyandrous marriages, where a woman could have two husbands essentially, none of them involved sexual relations.

Brian: Correct.

GT: That's your opinion. Ok. So let's talk a little bit about...

Brian: Rick, let me interrupt though. If people go to my books, they're going to be confused because I used the word eleven. The twelfth polyandrous marriage on the chart is Sarah Ann Whitney to Joseph C. Kingsbury, which was a front marriage. Everybody involved with that realized that she was sealed to Joseph but apparently there was some legal issues going on, so Joseph asked Kingsbury to have a legal marriage but not consummate the marriage. Everybody agrees that was the relationship. That's number twelve.

Number thirteen is Lucinda Pendleton who we just know nothing about, and the fourteenth one is to Mary Herron who we have one attestation that connects her to Joseph sexually but we don't know any of the details. If somebody goes to my chart, there's actually fourteen women on that but eleven of them we believe were eternity-only, two are undocumented so just take your guess, and then we have this pretend marriage with Sarah Ann, so fourteen in total.

GT: Oh, ok. Great. Well let's talk about, I believe it was Orson Hyde or Orson Pratt, I always get those two mixed up. One of them Joseph sent on a mission and then supposedly married his wife while he was on a mission. Can you talk about that story?

Brian: It's a great story. In 1842 John C. Bennett wrote a book called <u>History of the Saints</u>.[8] If we wanted to take a minute, I just bought an original copy of it. I have it upstairs for thousands of dollars.

GT: Oh my goodness!

Brian: It's got writing from 1842 in it. It's pretty exciting to me. In that book he says Joseph would send men on missions and marry their wives. Well of the fourteen women, we know that eleven of them, their husbands were not on missions. Two of the men, we don't have a date for the marriage so we can't say. The only one of them that we know was on a mission was Orson Hyde. Orson Hyde went to Palestine with the Twelve [Apostles.] We all know the story. Over a year later we have a sealing date between him and Orson Hyde's wife Marinda.

GT: Between Joseph and Marinda.

Brian nods: The problem is we have two sealing dates for Joseph and Marinda. The other date is from an affidavit Marinda signed that is well after Orson Hyde returning from Palestine. Even the one that appears to be a case where Joseph might have sent him on a mission, then he waits a year—it doesn't make sense. A year later we have Joseph being sealed to Marinda, but again we have a second date. The second date is a signed affidavit which we probably would consider to be more reliable than something that was just scrawled on a page in Joseph's journal, not in his handwriting but in I think Thomas Bullock's [handwriting.] Again that story is false,

---

[8] Can be purchased at http://amzn.to/2spKQdV

yet it's a sound bite. It's all over the internet. We've got to kill it. It's wrong. It's false. Joseph did not send men on missions and so he could marry their wives according to any reliable documentation.

GT: Hmmm. I've always heard that was reliable so that's interesting.

So he had fourteen potentially polyandrous marriages, he had the one with Fanny, what about the other, how many are there?

Brian: By my count he was sealed to 35. But by my dear wife's count it was 33, which corresponds to Todd Compton's 33. Todd had some additional possible wives and all. I don't think any of them, Mary Herron was on that list actually, but not Esther Dutcher.

{break}

GT: Let's go back to [D&C] 132 once again. I keep going back there. It does say that polygamy was around to raise up seed. Why do you think there were no offspring, or at least no known offspring of Joseph and a polygamist wife?

Brian: Again, it's a great question. I had theorized, and if you read my books you'll find there are two that I thought were Joseph's.

GT: Yeah, Josephine.

Brian: Josephine being one. We know by DNA that wasn't. The other one is, there's an account from Joseph Lee Robinson saying that Joseph and Olive Frost had a child. It was a single attestation, and I had discounted it. But then I heard an interview read between Joseph F. Smith and a guy named Whitehead. I'm blocking on his first name. He was a secretary to Joseph in Nauvoo. He arrived kind of late but he could write and helped out there, so he was close enough to know what was going

44

on. I heard the interview read. It hasn't been published even still.

I interpreted that as being Joseph had a wife Olive Frost and they had a child. Well since that was what I was going on when I wrote my book, the transcript of that interview has been released, and John Hajicek owns that, and he's a friend and allowed the transcript to come out. It's clear the child was between Olive and Brigham. Brigham Young married several of Joseph's wives after the martyrdom. The timeline only allows Brigham.

GT interrupts: Was that passed to you up at Mormon History [Meetings]?

Brian: Yeah!

GT interrupts: I remember that.

Brian: It came in on my phone as a text message from John. Because I said John, I really want to make sure what I'm saying here is accurate, and so he sent it to me, nice guy that he is. I was able to verify what I had already written up and made into slides as being accurate.

So we drop Olive's child. We don't even know the gender, because both she and the child died before they left Nauvoo. Then we take Josephine off the table and that just leaves accusations, and not a single documented child to Joseph. I think at least seven of them have been disproven through DNA. The others are pretty dubious.

I have a chart. It's at https://josephsmithspolygamy.org . It's at https://mormonpolygamydocuments.org as well. You can find it there where I've got them all listed there. It's like 20 accusations. What Don Bradley and I have done over the years is we've tried to trace these down. What we find is if a family can tie Joseph to be the father of some child, if he's anywhere within 50 miles of when this child is conceived, some of these families are just willing to accuse Joseph.

In one case there were people leaving the church because they were so appalled by the fact Joseph had this child. Then DNA comes out and shows Joseph isn't. Rumors can be very strong in families, and we have to be really careful with them. There's no documented children.

GT: Ok. You do hold, even with the polyandrous wives, you are saying there was probably no sexual relations. There were sexual relations with others, just no offspring.

Brian nods: Again in Appendix E, I compiled all of the evidences that had been available to that point. Of course it doesn't have the DNA now to disprove the one, but I show twelve possible evidences of sexuality with twelve of the wives. Some of the evidence is deposition level, signed attestation type of thing, and some of it is really dubious. But there's no evidence for more than twelve. Personally, I believe he probably had two that went by other names, and DNA...

GT interrupts: Two children.

Brian nods: Two children by the plural wives. There is one account by George A. Smith I think where he recounts how he came up to Joseph and the account is he approaches Joseph and he says, "What's up?" So I guess they had the same kind of conversational words here, "What's up?"

Joseph is washing his hands, saying that Emma served as a midwife for one of his plural wives had just delivered a baby. This very easily could have been, say between September of [18]43 and Joseph's death [in June 1844] because he has several plural wives living in Nauvoo Mansion under the watchful eye of Emma. We don't know anything about the dynamics of that home. I mean Emma could have kept them separate all the time or should could have allowed some interactions. We don't know.

If you want to look at a timeline, she may have felt ok about polygamy and allowed and participated in this as a midwife. Again it's speculation, but that account was repeated several times by, it wasn't George Albert Smith's—I'm blocking on which of the leader's—he was a polygamist—left this story. You put that with Mary Elizabeth Rollin's recollection of two or three children by Joseph's plural wives, what you find is scattered evidences from pretty good sources, but they're late, documenting had at least one, if not two or three children, but we have no idea who they are.

Joseph Smith's Youngest Teen Brides

Introduction

In the Gospel Topics essays on polygamy[9] at LDS.org, it says that Joseph Smith was married to a young girl who was "several months before her 15th birthday," meaning she was just 14 years old. She wasn't the only teenage bride that Joseph Smith had. We'll talk to Dr. Brian Hales about these sealings. Were there other ways that Joseph could have been sealed to these young women that didn't involve marriage?

The Interview

GT: The Gospel Topics essay references[10] someone who were under 15 I think, so they were 14 years old.

Brian: Ok, you're probably thinking of Helen Mar Kimball.

GT: Oh that's who I'm thinking of.

Brian: There are two 14-year-olds. The other 14-year-old was Nancy Maria Winchester. We don't know anything about that relationship, when it happened. She may have been 15; my bet is she was 14. Helen Mar Kimball is the one 14-year-old. For several reasons I don't believe that relationship was consummated, but Joseph gets accused of all kinds of crazy things. People even call him a pedophile.

---

[9] See https://www.lds.org/topics/plural-marriage-in-kirtland-and-nauvoo?lang=eng
[10] See https://www.lds.org/topics/plural-marriage-in-kirtland-and-nauvoo?lang=eng

Now a pedophile is someone who's interested in children under 11, which would not apply to Joseph in the wildest of rumors, but he was sealed to probably two 14-year-olds, and a 16-year-old.

GT: Was that Fanny, the 16-year-old?

Brian: No Fanny was, depending on when you want to date it, 17-19. By my dating she was 19.

GT: Ok.

Brian: Some people push it to [18]33 and she would have been 17. The 16-year-old was Flora Ann Woodworth. Actually Flora was divorced from Joseph. Most people don't know this. She had a blowup with Emma, Flora did. Joseph had given Flora a gold watch. Emma demanded the watch. We don't know how Emma found out about it. According to the very sketchy notes we have, Emma took the watch and smashed it, destroyed it under foot.

The next day after this confrontation, I'm indebted to William Clayton for some of these details for the timeline. Flora went out and married a non-member, Carlos Gove. There were conversations with Joseph and Flora and then Helen Mar was the one who reported that actually they separated. There's essentially a divorce between Joseph and Flora, which is the only one that we're aware of all of these. Flora later said he intended to cling to the prophet, suggesting that maybe it wasn't a full divorce, that maybe a for-time divorce or something. Again we're working with some sketchy details but the language would certainly support that.

Getting back to the 14-year-olds, we only know about Helen. Gratefully Helen lived a long time and she wrote

49

more supporting Joseph and plural marriage than any other woman in the church in the 19th century. Whatever happened with her and Joseph did not cause her to lose faith in Joseph or even plural marriage. But what we know from pretty good sources, from her primarily, was that her husband was Heber C. Kimball, and Heber C. Kimball wanted to please Joseph or create some kind of a family bond, so Heber C. Kimball taught Helen, and then offered Helen, according to Helen's word, like a ewe-lamb to Joseph, and Joseph taught her plural marriage and agreed to be sealed.

You could say, why didn't Joseph just tell her to wait? We don't know the answer to that, but what we can piece together from what Helen wrote, the sealing occurred, and after the sealing, Helen continued to go to dances and balls and socialize for the next several months until at one point Joseph stepped in and said, Look. We don't want her doing this anymore.

Later Helen said that she hated polygamy. She wrote this down early on. This was one of the early writings before she wrote her books defending it. But the reason why she hated polygamy was not because of her own relationship with it, but because of how it affected her mother. I argue that if she were having conjugal relations with Joseph and finding that to be undesirable, she might have actually used her relationship with Joseph as a reason for hating polygamy.

{break}

GT: I know there's a story in Nauvoo where Emma offered Jane Manning James [See our discussion about Jane in Part 1[11] and Part 2[12]],

---

[11] See https://wp.me/p8l6gx-5S
[12] See https://wp.me/p8l6gx-62

a black servant in the Smith household to be adopted as a daughter. Why do you think they didn't offer the same thing with Helen Mar Kimball?

Brian: Do you know there were no adoptions performed during Joseph's lifetime. The only adoptions that we have any record of occurred in the Nauvoo Temple and they occurred around, depending on your definition of an adoption, there's 205 or something. A lot of these, I use the word adoption to mean a child is sealed to parents who they are not biologically related.

GT: Right. I know John D. Lee was sealed to Brigham as a son even though John was older than Brigham.

Brian: Right.

GT: But that was after the Nauvoo period.

Brian: Actually John D. Lee was the only non-church leader who went into the Nauvoo Temple and had non-relatives sealed to him as their children. There are like 22 men and women. He got this idea, and it persisted for several years, that you gain some eternal advantage if you have more children either biologically or through adoption. So he put all these people together, they were all in this company. This is all brand new stuff.   The leaders are going, we don't know about adoption because it didn't happen from Joseph. I don't think Joseph really told them much about it and they're just figuring it out as they go. What's interesting is that within a year or two, all of these relationships had asked Brigham to have it be broken off.

John D. Lee was thinking these "children" were going to be taking care of him as their parent, and all of these children were thinking John D. Lee was going to take care

51

of them, as his children. So when it finally came out, nobody wanted to be part of John D. Lee's family. My understanding is, and I haven't researched it in detail, but I think they all left John D. Lee.

Of course once the Nauvoo Temple was closed, there were no adoption sealings. Now Dick Bennett and I were together just a week ago. We laughed a little because he and I have been on opposite sides. Well were there sealings in Winter Quarters? He said there was, probably. I'm saying, I don't think you can do that outside of a temple. Brigham was very explicit that you couldn't do those outside of a temple, so the adoption issue is something that wasn't available in Nauvoo, to answer your question. {To learn more of the Law of Adoption, see Dr. Dick Bennett's interview[13]}

GT: Ok, so you're saying that just in, and I don't know when Helen Mar Kimball was sealed to Joseph, but that just really wasn't an option in that year to be sealed as a child rather than as a wife?

Brian: Well they didn't have a temple, and you can't do adoption sealings outside of a temple.

GT: Adoption sealings, ok, so therefore it had to be a plural marriage....

Brian: Right.

GT: ...because that could be done outside the temple.

Brian: Right.

GT: Oh really!

---

[13] See https://gospeltangents.com/2017/04/13/sealing-to-gas-through-law-of-adoption/

Brian: Yeah. I call them horizontal marriages, husband and wife. Those sealings can be done outside of a temple, but they're supposed to be done again either by proxy or by the same people again in the temple. But they are valid outside when you have one.

But the vertical sealing of a child to parent can only be done in a temple setting. While there's some questionable things with John Bernhisle and perhaps some others in Winter Quarters, I think they were really consistent in that, and Brigham only allowed it, and so none of them occurred until 1877. They had the Endowment House in Utah in Salt Lake. They did not perform any adoptions. Dick and I agreed on that. {See Dick Bennett's discussion of the Law of Adoption.[14]}

GT: But there were some adoptive sealings in Nauvoo before they left west.

Brian: Right. But it's also confusing because in the months and years after that, there was a lot of talk about people increasing their kingdoms on earth, but all they could do was get promises of families to be in George Albert Smith's family, or in Parley Pratt's family or somebody else, Willard Richards family. So there was a period of time where there was this idea that these men were getting some eternal advantage and so were the people that were in their families. But these things were not sealed in an ordinance in the temple. These were just promises, most of which just were forgotten because it was many years later that they were able to do the adoption ordinances in the St. George Temple.

---

[14] See https://gospeltangents.com/2017/04/13/sealing-to-gas-through-law-of-adoption/

Polygamy & the Temple Lot Case

Introduction

The Temple Lot Case is one of the most important sources documents for polygamy for Mormon historians. Back in the late 1800s, the RLDS Church claimed Joseph was a monogamist and wanted to own the temple lot in Independence, Missouri. However, another group known as Temple Lot Mormons colloquially—actually they are called the Church of Christ (Temple Lot) owned the property. They wanted to retain ownership of this. The LDS Church decided to help the Temple Lot Mormons and had women testify about their polygamist relationships to Joseph Smith. Dr. Brian Hales describes their testimony and why this is such an important court case. We'll continue our conversation talking about Helen Mar Kimball and why she was or wasn't involved in the Temple Lot Case. Check out our conversation...

The Interview

Brian: After the sealing, Helen continued to go to dances and balls and socialize for the next several months until at one point Joseph stepped in and said, Look. We don't want her doing this anymore.

Later Helen said that she hated polygamy. She wrote this down early on. This was one of the early writings before she wrote her books defending it. But the reason she hated polygamy was not because of her own relationship with it, but because of how it affected her mother. I argue that if she were having conjugal relations with Joseph and finding that to be undesirable, she might have actually used her relationship with Joseph as a reason for hating polygamy.

But the real question that comes up is if the marriage was consummated, and I don't think it was, why did they not call Helen to be a witness in the 1892 Temple Lot Case? I don't know if you're familiar with that.

GT: Talk about that.

Brian: It's kind of a fun little episode. Let me digress for just a minute because Don Bradley pointed this out at one point. He's written an article on it. If it had not been for the RLDS Church, they started in 1860 and they had two primary issues. One was that the president of the church had to be genetically related to Joseph Smith, and so Joseph Smith III, his son was the first president of the RLDS Church. But their other big thing was Joseph wasn't a polygamist.

So they started sending missionaries out to Utah in the late 1860s and through the 1870s. What did the church do? The LDS Church in Salt Lake decided we're going to document what happened back in Nauvoo because nobody was writing about it almost. So in 1869 Joseph F. Smith collected dozens of affidavits, other stories, testimonials, all this stuff was collected. Why? To counter the claims of the RLDS Church. [In] 1877, Andrew Jensen is an independent researcher, collects all these stories. He didn't know about the 1869 affidavits, so he creates this other cache of accounts talking about Nauvoo polygamy. Then in 1892 we find this lawsuit. What was happening was the Hedrickites, they like to be called Church of Christ (Temple Lot), but they followed originally this guy named Hedrick.

GT: Granville Hedrick.

Brian: Yeah, and they owned the temple lot. They physically were there, and the RLDS Church had just gained possession of the Kirtland Temple by suing the people that were living in it, or owned it, by saying we are the original church so we still own it. Even though they really didn't prevail, is my understanding, in the court, because the winners of the Kirtland Temple....

GT: Kirtland or Independence?

Brian: I'm talking Kirtland now, because it segues into Independence.

GT: Yeah because the Hedrickites are in Independence, right?

Brian: Right, right.

GT: Because I'm a little confused there.

Brian: Sorry, it's good to clarify. But in Kirtland my understanding is the lawsuit, the RLDS Church lost it. But they read the decision by the judge, and they ran out of the court yelling "we won! We won!" They just pushed the owners who actually had won the suit out, and just took possession of it. Because the people who won the suit and were in possession didn't understand that they had won it. So they just kind of by default took over the Kirtland Temple.

GT: The Temple Lot people, the Hedrickites took over the Kirtland Temple?

Brian: No, this is the RLDS Church. The RLDS Church wanted to start getting ownership of these places so they sued the people who owned the Kirtland Temple. They lost but they said they won and they took possession of it. So their next quest was to take possession of the Independence lot. Well that was a little different because at this point the Utah church didn't want them to win. There was a lot of animosity between the two groups: the RLDS [Church] and the Utah church.

So even though the Hedrickites did not practice polygamy, the Utah church helped the Hedrickites prove, or attempt to prove that Joseph Smith taught polygamy. Polygamy was part of the original church, and the RLDS Church doesn't practice polygamy so they aren't the same church as Joseph Smith organized. Does that make sense?

GT agrees: Uh huh.

Brian: It's a little complicated, but that was the primary argument: polygamy was the major issue in all of the discussion. If the RLDS Church is the same church, then they've got to prove Joseph wasn't a polygamist, so we have several accounts. They're very late, giving us additional details about Nauvoo polygamy. If we didn't have the RLDS Church saying Joseph wasn't a polygamist, we wouldn't have the 1869 affidavits, we wouldn't have the 1887 collection by Andrew Jensen, and we wouldn't have the additional information from the Temple Lot Case. Together those three are 75% of what we know, and it's scary for a researcher on polygamy to think about what we would know about Nauvoo polygamy if the RLDS Church had not taken the stance that they did. It's really scary. You'd have John C. Bennett. You'd have William Law, and you would not know even a fraction of what we think we know about it today.

So what happened in the Temple Lot case, this is 1892, the Hedrickites and the RLDS show up with their attorneys, and they're taking depositions of LDS Church members that are helping the Hedrickites, saying Joseph was a polygamist. The RLDS Church is not the same church. Joseph had nine plural wives that were still living. Three of them had been polyandrous wives. They were not called. Why is that?

Was the church too embarrassed about polyandry, or was it because these were eternity only marriages that were non-sexual and wouldn't have done anything to help the Hedrickites case? The Hedrickites wanted to prove Joseph was a full-fledged polygamist with sexual relations in some of his marriages. Well they did call three wives. All three of them testified that they had sexual relations with Joseph.

GT: Three wives that were not polyandrous.

Brian: Not polyandrous. There were nine total, three were polyandrous, were not called, three of them were called. What's interesting, they all testified of having relations with Joseph. But Helen Mar Kimball was not called. She was one of the three that weren't called, and yet she lived very close to where the depositions were being taken. She could have gone down there. She knew about them. It's in the journal. Her journal talks about them being in town and doing this.

My argument is that the reason they didn't call Helen wasn't because she was 14 and they would have been embarrassed. I mean a 14-year-old marriage was eyebrow raising but it wasn't scandalous in Nauvoo. I would think even in Utah in 1890. But the real reason was that Helen could not say that she had relations with Joseph. This was just an unconsummated sealing at that point just like the polyandrous ones.

So that's why these four women were not called. The three that they did call were very pointed. "Did you have carnal intercourse with Joseph?" I mean the language would have made them terribly uncomfortable because these were Victorian women, embracing a very conservative belief system, and they would not have liked to talk about it, but they did.

When I put all these pieces together, that Joseph did not seek the marriage with Helen. He did go along. He didn't seek it. By several evidences, I don't believe it was consummated. These claims that Joseph was going after these 14-year-olds is really not sustained from a documentary standpoint.

Emma Denied Joseph Practiced Polygamy?

Introduction

The RLDS Church was founded on the claim that Joseph Smith never practiced polygamy. Even on her death bed, Emma Smith made the startling claim to some that Joseph never practiced polygamy. Conservative bloggers such as Rock Waterman (see his post here[15]) and even Denver Snuffer have made the claim that Joseph Smith was a monogamist. However, current RLDS Church prophet/president Stephen Veazey has made the claim[16] that historical records show that Joseph Smith did practice polygamy. What does Dr. Brian Hales believe about these allegations about monogamy and Joseph Smith?

The Interview

GT: Let's talk about Emma again. As I understand it on her death bed, she said that Joseph never practiced polygamy. Why do you think she denied that? Was that just she didn't want to believe it or she didn't want her children to believe it?

Brian: You know just months before she died, Joseph Smith III asked her a series of questions. It took several days to get these answers recorded. They were recorded by Joseph Smith III. In that set of questions, she said some things that are really important historically. This is where we learn about Joseph Smith dictating the Book of Mormon, and then taking a break and coming back, starting off right where he left off, and details that we hold to be very important.

---

[15] See http://puremormonism.blogspot.com/2010/06/why-im-abandoning-polygamy.html

[16] See https://mormonheretic.org/2009/06/04/amazing-coc-statement/

Well one of the questions was, was Joseph a polygamist? She denies that he had any other wives than her. There has been some theories that she may have had some senility and just meant it but had forgotten. That's Mark Staker's take on it.

GT: Oh.

Brian: He shared that with me, and it will be in a book that he's working on. Lawrence Foster who you also quoted, a very good polygamy scholar. He theorizes that the questions were phrased so that there could be plausible denial. In other words, you're going to deny polygamy but it's not talking about celestial marriage. As I look at the questions I don't really see that parsing of words to allow that but Larry is a smart guy and that's how he rationalizes Emma's denial.

I have an article that I have been pitching to different people to publish on the denials. To be quite honest with you, there are at least two other denials that clearly were not senility, were clearly not specially phrased questions where Emma just comes right out and they're fairly well documented, said "Joseph did not practice polygamy."

How do I deal with that? I don't know. I do not have a good explanation. I think Emma was an amazing woman. I look forward to meeting her someday. You know in our theology that's a possibility. She had the worst row to hoe of all the polygamist wives in my view. She did remarkably well. She stumbled, but I believe there's plenty of forgiveness on these things for her, but I honestly don't know how she was able to say these things that she said. Hopefully these will be published. I've put them together, I just haven't got them published yet. It's pretty clear that she just denied it flat out. I don't know how she made that work for her, but they're there.

GT: There's another book, Joseph Fought Polygamy,[17] by the Prices.

Brian points at his bookshelf: It's right over there. It's on my shelf. {both chuckle}

GT: I would assume they would probably quote Emma quite a bit as well. I've been surprised. I know Rock Waterman is somebody who has bought into this.[18] It boggles my mind why anybody would say that Joseph never practiced polygamy. Talk about what are some of the justifications for that, and then why are those justifications incorrect.

Brian: You know it's interesting, Rick, that you would bring that up because by the time this interview is aired, *The Interpreter* {a Mormon history journal} will have published a very long article[19] that I have written where I don't just give evidence that Joseph did it, but I actually attack the arguments by, I mention Rock Waterman, I mention the Prices, and then Denver Snuffer who is in my view just the latest false prophet. Remember I started looking at Mormon fundamentalism and I documented and wrote articles on men or came as great leaders who came for this reason or that reason and then they just fall by the wayside. There's a number of these that I talk about in my book. I think Denver is just the latest in all of this type of a pattern.

For those who have questions, the easiest way probably to detect Denver is he said Joseph didn't practice polygamy, and then just look at the evidence. I outline it

---

[17] Can be purchased at http://amzn.to/2tbi3tT
[18] See http://puremormonism.blogspot.com/2010/06/why-im-abandoning-polygamy.html
[19] See http://www.mormoninterpreter.com/joseph-smith-monogamist-or-polygamist/

all here. It is true that most of the evidence that Joseph practiced plural marriage is from late sources, but not all of it. *The Nauvoo Expositor* states right in there that Joseph Smith had a revelation. It was read to the high council. We've got testimonials from William Law and Jane Law saying that Joseph was teaching polygamy. These are contemporaneous. There are entries in William Clayton's journal. John C. Bennett clearly had heard some rumors. I don't know that he was ever in confidence of Joseph with it. But to say that it's all old is not true. There are some very important contemporaneous sources.

Then you've got a whole truckload of late sources from dozens and dozens of people who must have been in a huge conspiracy, or Joseph was practicing it and actively teaching it. I also in that have a section on section 132. People say it was doctored up or something like that. It is true that the William Clayton version was destroyed. We don't know exactly how. There's contradictory evidences there. Did Emma burn it, or did she insist that Joseph burn it? I mean the differences are not huge but it clearly was destroyed.

There had been a copy made, and this is by Joseph C. Kingsbury. He did it. He was a penman. He could write it. In that day if you could write with a good pen, a good handwriting, that set you apart because not everybody was that literate in the Nauvoo era. He wrote this down at Bishop Whitney's request and he kept that. This is Helen's father. He kept it in a notebook until 1847 when he was asked to give this to Brigham.

We have an account from Horace Whitney who wrote it down, copied it and that copy they still have I guess. I don't know, but the copy that Joseph C. Kingsbury wrote down is available online. You can find it on the Joseph Smith Papers Project.[20] I've reposted it too. But it you look at it, it's clearly in Kingsbury's hand. It's not been doctored up. There's no evidence that anybody was editing it or making changes in it or anything like the accusations are saying. We've got testimonies from Clayton and Kingsbury that this is the actual document that Joseph dictated that day. It dates back to 1843. The provenance is very good. The idea that Brigham had it written up is not something supported by any kind of evidence.

This is the first time anybody has actually written down a provenance of the Kingsbury copy. There may be some details we wish we had but it's really pretty clear that Whitney kept it until 1847, then Brigham had it and he published it in 1853. To try to bring in some other scenario to support Denver Snuffer's version or something, it's a contrivance. There's just no way to do it from historical documentation standpoint in my view.

GT: Ok. So you mentioned as far as the revelation, do you think Joseph had an idea that Emma would throw that in the fire so that's why they made two copies of section 132?

Brian: I think it's a coincidence that there was a second copy made. The accounts don't say Joseph was pushing for this. Hyrum was involved, but they wanted this copy and so they just allowed it to happen, so then there were two copies running around, and we have numerous accounts from people saying they saw it. They read the copy, and we can't ever tell, was it the Clayton copy and this had been destroyed or was it the Kingsbury copy. My guess is most of these accounts are talking about the

---

[20] See http://www.josephsmithpapers.org/

Clayton copy before it was destroyed because the Kingsbury copy was not.

GT: So Clayton wrote a copy. Kingsbury wrote a copy, and the Clayton copy got thrown in the fire by Emma. The Kingsbury copy stayed.

Brian: Right.

GT: That's very interesting. Since you mentioned Denver Snuffer. I read his book [Passing the Heavenly Gift[21]]. In his book he mentioned that he thought that D&C 132 was actually four different revelations received at different times, and essentially Brigham Young conflated them all together. There was eternal marriage, which was basically monogamous. Then there's the polygamy revelation if I'm remembering this right. Then there's the message to Emma where it says if you don't accept this you're going to be destroyed, and I'm trying to remember what the fourth one was. What is your opinion on that? Do you think that's true that this could have been four separate revelations that were conflated together in a single revelation?

Brian: Well the idea that the revelation can be divided into three or four sections is not new. People have been saying that for decades. The way that you divided it up is quite exact. If you go up, you have eternal marriage mentioned up until about [verse] 32, then there's some discussion about polygamy, old time polygamy, Old Testament polygamy. Then we launch in, I think it's around verse 51 to Emma that takes up the next fifteen verses.

GT: Seven verses.

Brian: Well you could actually divide it at verse 61 but she's mentioned again in verse 64 so those are the first three or four divisions that are typically made. We don't

[21] See http://amzn.to/2rRPrly

know when they were received, but by every account we have it was dictated from verse one to 66. You've got to start speculating and making up a history if you want to say that part of it was dictated here, another part was made up here, and then it came together. There's just nothing to support that historically. Clayton said he wrote it down completely.

GT: In one session.

Brian: Kingsbury, in one session. It's in his journal, it's in Joseph's journal. There's contemporaneous evidence in two places that a revelation was written on July 12, 1843 and it dealt with polygamy. Then you've got the Kingsbury copy which goes from beginning to end. People can make up their own historical fictions, but if we make those the basis for a belief system, we're going to get into trouble. If you want to disagree with me or with this account, that's great but bring some evidence. Everybody wins. We may not agree at the end of it, but at least we'll be looking at documents that can help us find the truth rather than just speculations that come out of the air as near as I can tell.

Brian Hales Role with the Gospel Topics Essays

The Interview

GT: Are you working on any other books or projects that you'd like to share with us?

Brian: Well actually, yes I am. I've kind of shifted gears. I had somebody ask me just last week, it was Chris Smith. You know Chris. He's got his Ph.D., nice guy. He said, "are you still writing on polygamy?"

I paused for a minute. I thought, "You know I don't know what more there is to write." I'd love to write some more on polyandry. Dan Vogel and I have been having a public disagreement on that topic. There's no new evidence. He's not brought forth any, and I don't have any really to offer, some of the things I alluded to here. I'd love to see some new things come out on polyandry and I would write on that, but pretty much I think that everything that can be said without new evidence has kind of been said.

The thing that I would add as a response to your question, Rick, is that I've never been really been comfortable with the naturalist's explanation of the text of the Book of Mormon. If you can see up here, maybe you can't but there's all these versions of the Book of Mormon up here, the different printings year by year and if you look at the naturalist view, it's just that Joseph got up one day and started to dictate this text, the 116 pages. Then there's a pause and we go to Oliver Cowdery shows up and then over a period of just a few weeks, he dictates 273,725 words by my count of the Book of Mormon text; that's the 1830 version.

I've just never been comfortable that Joseph could have dictated that and so I've been investigating the different theories about that. I've written an article I hope to have published. In this article, what I did is I compared Joseph to other 24 year old or younger authors who wrote big books and I compared their education. I compared their word counts and the complexity of their books. When you line them all up, 24 years and older—Joseph was 23 when he dictated it but it was published a year later when he was 24. I have to use the publishing dates of these other books because they are obviously written before. The biggest book written by anybody 24 or younger is about 180,000. Joseph's book is almost 50% longer.

GT: 180,000 words?

Brian: 180,000 words versus 273,000. Then when you look at the complexity—in fact I've got them on the shelf here somewhere. One of the books is just really simplistic. I tried to read it but it's just—I couldn't get into it. It's written for like a seventh grader or an eighth grader, but it's 180,000 words. Then there's a series by a guy named Christopher Paolini—the Eragon[22] Series, it's an independent series it's called. He wrote two books that were very long before the age of 24.

But again when you get into the text, it's just pretty simplistic stuff. I mean the names and everything are very, very different, not nearly as complex. There's no chiasmus or stylometric issues like with the Book of Mormon. So Joseph Smith is just curiously unique as an author of this Book of Mormon. So I'm focusing not only on the word count, but also on the way it was presented because the numbers don't lie.

---

[22] Can be purchased at http://amzn.to/2sgU9bM

When people want to say Tolkien wrote a book and that's just like Joseph writing the Book of Mormon or Shakespeare had all of these plays that are very complex, and that's just like Joseph Smith, when you get into the details, Joseph is unique. There is no one like Joseph who had come up with a book like the Book of Mormon. That's what the evidence is showing. In fact when I was putting this chart together, I actually posted it on ex-Mormon Reddit. I thought, if there's something wrong with this...

GT: You'll get feedback there!

Brian: because the Book of Mormon is way out. It's just different. Whatever you want to say the reasons are, Joseph as an author at age 23, 24 of the Book of Mormon—he's different from any other author that I could identify. They actually found one other author that was important, it was Paolini, but there's still nothing there. So I'll be interested on the critics' view of these articles and things when they come out that I'm working on. Believe me it's so much nicer than working on the controversial polygamy. I'm very happy to just be having fun with the Book of Mormon and how it has come forth.

GT: That's cool. I just remembered two more questions that I wanted to ask you.

Brian: Ok.

GT: The Gospel Topics essay, I've seen a blog post, I guess Elder Marlin Jensen recently said that basically they commissioned a bunch of scholars to write a big essay, then the church would kind of condensed those down. I was just wondering, did you have anything to do with those Gospel Topics essays on polygamy[23]?

---

[23] See http://bit.ly/1wAFchl

Brian: Yeah, I gave them a very long essay, and then maybe a couple of years later they sent me the Gospel Topics essay that was similar to what we have today. I went through it all. I think we had one other meeting in the interim, maybe two. I just went through and made recommendations on it, and every recommendation I recommended in the text they accepted. There were some outside comments that I made some recommendations they did not, but they were very generous to allow me to do that. They do quote from the trilogy a number of times and an article I wrote was also referenced.

GT: So that took a few years for that whole process to go through?

Brian: Yeah, you know originally they were thinking of doing long answer, medium answer, short answer. That was the first thing that was asked of me on the topic of polyandry. Then I just sent them some general stuff, and I don't know how many iterations it went through there. Again I was excited to contribute to that. I only looked at the Nauvoo material. I know they had Kathryn Daines help out, and Kathleen Flake I think also are the other two that did the input on plural marriage. I hope they don't mind me saying that but they wanted outsiders to critique it. If there were problems, they wanted to know about them before they published it.

GT: Of course! Cool. Then my last question was, I know you're an active Latter-day Saint. You used to sing in the Tabernacle Choir. I always told my wife. My wife has a big goal that she would like to sing in there.

Brian: Oh, good luck.

GT: Anyway, I'm just curious. Do your ward members know that you've written this big three volume set[24], and do they ever ask you questions or do they just not care?

Brian: You know most of them don't know. We were at a ward party one time and we were sitting by some younger couples that I didn't know because they had just split our ward, or rearranged the ward boundaries and there was a young gal sitting right across from me and she was, "Wait, you're Brian Hales!"

She was really surprised. She had run into my CES Letter material because I've got a website that I think exposes the CES letter.[25] She was surprised that way. But overall, I think most of them don't know. Craig Foster who is also a polygamy scholar, especially on fundamentalism, he's in my ward. We were just talking on Sunday and we just said, nobody in here really knows we're doing all this controversial stuff. The bishop knows and our stake president knows, and of course they are very supportive.

What I tell people is if you don't have a problem with polygamy then just don't worry about it. I mean it's hard to make polygamy make you feel good because of how unfair it is on earth. I don't even tell them about my books because it can create questions and things. If their faith is good without it then I don't think they need to know every nuance about what's happening historically.

On the other hand, I do advise people to inoculate themselves and their families so that the first place, if they see it on the internet, they say, oh yeah, I know about that. I'll plug my wife's book, A Reason for Faith,[26]

---

[24] Can be purchased at http://amzn.to/2siGWUR
[25] See http://debunking-cesletter.com/

17 chapters each by an expert on all of the controversies in the church. I highly recommend that. People buy that A Reason for Faith. It comes in a CD as well.

Paul Reeve, who you've interviewed,[27] he wrote a chapter on race and priesthood. Laura and I did two chapters on polygamy. There's the Book of Abraham, Kinderhook plates, homosexuality. Richard Bushman did a chapter on treasure digging, so at least if you've read a book like that, and it's not a big book. It's an easy read. At least you're kind of inoculated to these kinds of things so if you have a question, you don't have to panic. Oh yeah, I never heard of that.

GT: So does the bishop and the stake president ever send people your way and say, "straighten these people out." {chuckles}

Brian: Actually we meet with quite a few people.

GT: Oh really?

Brian: Some of them come with faith and we can give answers, and then they go away happier. I mean it isn't an easy click your fingers, I'm doing better thing. But we always tell people, just keep learning. Be transparent. Learn everything. Don't give up until you've learned. You don't have to give up faith today. Find out what's going on. You can read the anti's but read the answers. Read the responses.

Other times when Laura and I meet with people, it's just I think a box that they have to check as they're on their way out of the church. "Oh yeah I met with the Hales.

[26] Can be purchased at http://amzn.to/2tlp3nx
[27] See https://gospeltangents.com/2017/02/09/how-mormons-became-a-racial-category/

They didn't help." So they've kind of already given up their faith.

The only thing I would say is if you've got questions, dive in. I believe there's somebody in the church who knows more about it than the person who wrote whatever you're reading on the internet and they still believe. With respect to plural marriage, we certainly have read a lot. It strengthened my belief in Joseph. It didn't make me like polygamy. I don't. I never want to do it, but my belief in him as a true prophet has just been strengthened.

GT: Great. Alright, well thank you so much. I really appreciate this time that you've spent here with me on *Gospel Tangents*. If I have any more questions can I call you again?

Brian: Sure! {Both chuckle} That's great.

GT: Alright, thanks a lot.

Brian: Thank you Rick.

GT: We'll see you.

Epilogue

I really appreciate Brian for taking time to talk with us and hope you learned as much as I did. This won't be our last conversation about polygamy. I have interviews scheduled with DNA expert Ugo Perego, modern polygamy expert Anne Wilde, and Jim Vun Cannon[28], Counselor in First Presidency of the Remnant Church of Jesus Christ of Latter Day Saints. (He says Joseph was a monogamist.)

I hope you'll tune in for our next conversation with David Rosenvall as we his unusual theory of Book of Mormon geography on the Baja Peninsula![29] For more information, please subscribe to our website https://GospelTangents.com. You can also get a transcript at Amazon.com.[30] Please subscribe to iTunes, Stitcher, or YouTube to get updated interviews. Thanks again for listening, and we hope you'll continue to support us here at Gospel Tangents!

---

[28] See https://gospeltangents.com/2017/07/27/found-literal-descendant-aaron/
[29] See https://gospeltangents.com/2017/07/12/book-mormon-baja-peninsula/
[30] See http://amzn.to/2mai9i2

Additional Resources:

Here are links to the blog so you can join the conversation, as well as videos of the interview.

Part 1 – Canadian Polygamy – Should it be Legal?
See: https://gospeltangents.com/2017/06/09/canadian-polygamy-should-it-be-legal/

Part 2 – Does Polygamy in D&C 132 conflict with JST Genesis?
See:

Part 3 – Declaration on Marriage – Polygamy Rumors
See:

Part 4 – 1st Plural Wife Fanny Alger: Time or Eternity?
See:

Part 5 – Fanny Alger Part 2: Plural Marriage or Adultery?
See:

Part 6 – What are the Theological Justifications of Polygamy?
See:

Part 7 – Mormon Polyandry: More than One Husband
See:

Part 8 – Joseph's Youngest Teen Brides
See:

Part 9 – Polygamy & the Temple Lot Case
See:

Part 10 – Emma Denied Joseph Practiced Polygamy?
See:

Part 11 – Did Brian Hales Write the Gospel Topics Essays?
See:

Here are Brian's books on *Joseph Smith's Polygamy*.

Volume 1, **See:** http://amzn.to/2qOlrq2

Volume 2, **See:** http://amzn.to/2sF3v1q

Volume 3: Theology , **See:** http://amzn.to/2qVygOw

Here's another conversation about Kirtland-era polygamy with Dr. Mark Staker.

Kirtland Era Polygamy
See: https://gospeltangents.com/2017/03/07/kirtland-era-polygamy/

Elijah's Visit & Sealing Keys
See: https://gospeltangents.com/2017/03/18/elijahs-visit-the-sealing-keys/

We'd also love to have you visit our Amazon Store on our website to see other books on Black LDS History, and other Mormon topics. Be sure to check out our blog as well at https://GospelTangents.com to find information about future guests and projects we are working on. We would also like to partner with artists and musicians to produce a documentary on this and other topics. Please email us at GospelTangents@gmail.com if you're interested.

Thank you for your generous support!

Thank you for your generous support!

www.ingramcontent.com/pod-product-compliance
Lightning Source LLC
Chambersburg PA
CBHW030859310526
45786CB00019B/2523